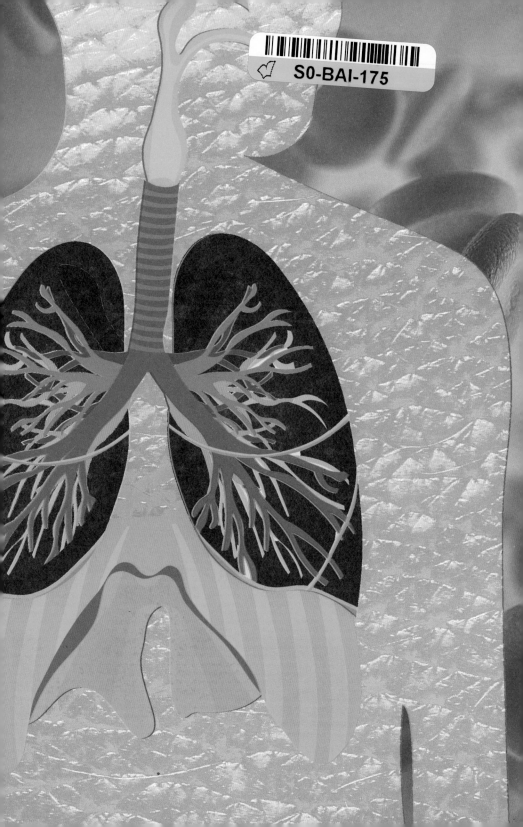

Amazing
Human Body

Written by Katherine Sully
Reading consultants: Alan Howe and Christopher Collier,
Bath Spa University, UK

This edition published by Parragon Books Ltd in 2013 and distributed by

Parragon Inc.
440 Park Avenue South, 13th Floor
New York, NY 10016
www.parragon.com

Edited by; Grace Harvey
Designed by; Francesca Winterman and Jess Tyrell
Production by; Joanne Knowlson

ISBN 978-1-4723-3026-0

Printed in China

DISCOVERY KIDS™

Amazing Human Body

PaRragon

Bath • New York • Singapore • Hong Kong • Cologne • Delhi
Melbourne • Amsterdam • Johannesburg • Shenzhen

Put on your 3D glasses and discover the workings of the human body. The body parts look so real, you will want to reach out and touch them!

Parents' Notes

This book is part of a series of nonfiction books designed to appeal to children learning to read. Each book has been developed with the help of educational experts.

At the end of the book is a quiz to help your child remember the information and the meanings of some of the words and sentences. Difficult words, which appear in bold in the book, can be found in the glossary at the back. There is also an index.

Contents

Your Body

The human body is made up of cells, tissues, organs, and organ systems that let you breathe, move, see, hear, and think.

Cells are like your body's building blocks. They are so tiny that you can only see them under a **microscope**.

When cells group together, they form **tissues** such as muscle.

The brain

When tissues group together, they form **organs** such as the heart and the brain.

A group of organs that work together to perform a special job is called an organ system. The group of organs that allows us to digest food is called the digestive system.

The heart

An adult body
is made up of
100 trillion cells!

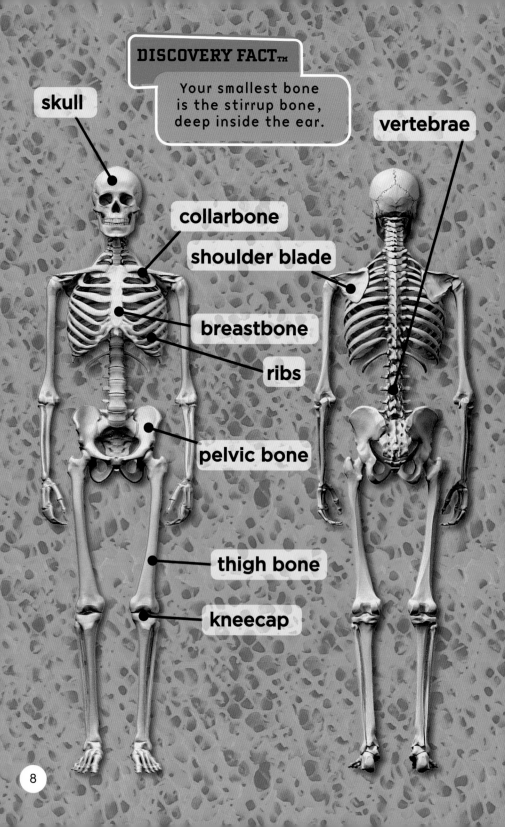

DISCOVERY FACT™

Your smallest bone is the stirrup bone, deep inside the ear.

skull

vertebrae

collarbone

shoulder blade

breastbone

ribs

pelvic bone

thigh bone

kneecap

Bones

Your skeleton holds up your body—without it, you would be a blob!

An adult skeleton is made up of 206 bones.

Your skeleton protects your **internal organs**. The skull protects the brain, and the ribs protect the heart, lungs, and liver.

Bones are hard on the outside and spongy on the inside. As you grow, they grow, too.

The place where two bones are connected is called a joint.

Knee joints

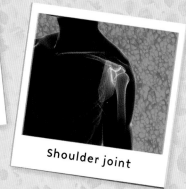

Shoulder joint

Muscles

Most muscles are attached to bones by stretchy **tendons**. Muscles work with your bones to make your body move.

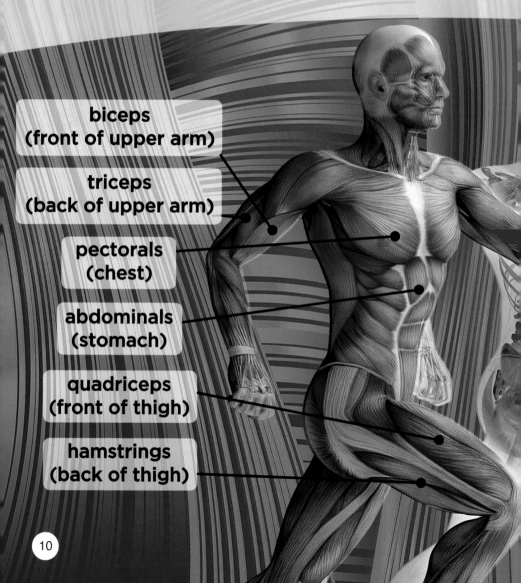

biceps
(front of upper arm)

triceps
(back of upper arm)

pectorals
(chest)

abdominals
(stomach)

quadriceps
(front of thigh)

hamstrings
(back of thigh)

To bend your elbow, the muscle at the front of your upper arm gets shorter, and the muscle at the back gets longer.

To straighten your elbow, the muscle at the back of your upper arm gets shorter, and the muscle at the front gets longer.

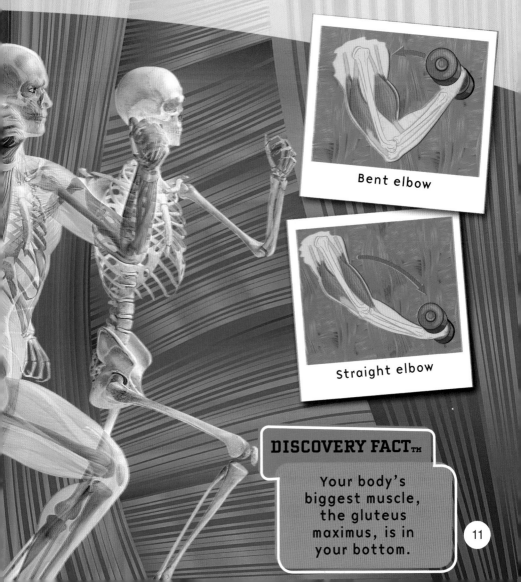

Bent elbow

Straight elbow

11

Breathing and Lungs

You breathe in and puff out air 15 to 25 times a minute. This is because your body needs to take **oxygen** from the air to stay alive.

A large muscle, called the diaphragm, is under your lungs.

When your diaphragm tightens, your lungs get bigger. This pulls air in.

When your diaphragm relaxes, your lungs get smaller. This pushes air out.

In the lungs, oxygen from the breathed-in air is **absorbed** into the blood.

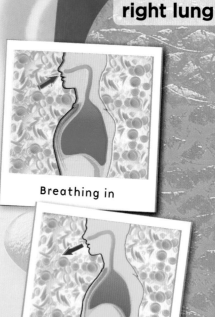

right lung

Breathing in

Breathing out

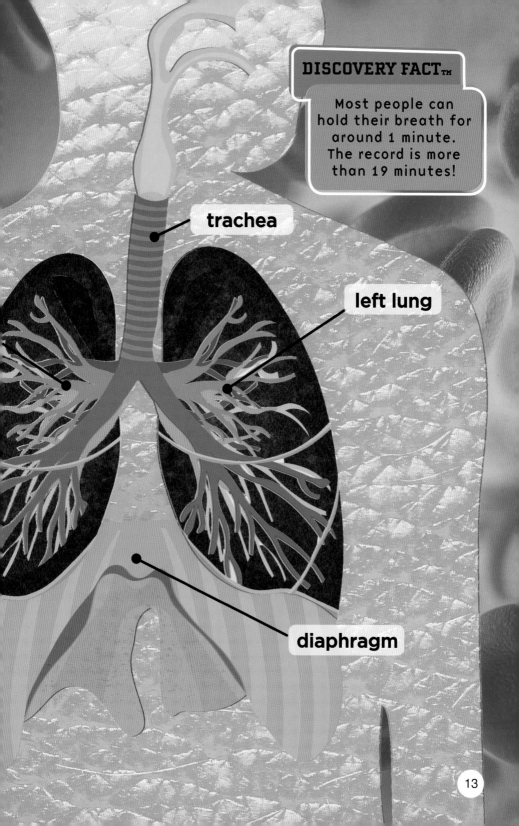

DISCOVERY FACT™

Most people can hold their breath for around 1 minute. The record is more than 19 minutes!

trachea

left lung

diaphragm

13

Blood and Heart

Your heart is a muscle made up of two pumps. It has a very important job to do. It beats nonstop, pumping blood around your body.

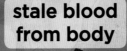

stale blood
from body

fresh blood
to body

stale blood
to lungs

fresh blood
from lungs

The right side of your heart pumps stale blood to your lungs, to collect **oxygen**.

The left side of your heart pumps fresh blood around your body, to deliver oxygen to your body parts.

white blood cells

Veins and arteries

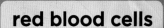

red blood cells

DISCOVERY FACT™

Tubes called arteries (in red) carry fresh blood away from the heart, and tubes called veins (in blue) carry stale blood to the heart.

The Senses

Your brain needs information from your **sense organs** in order for you to see, hear, smell, taste, and feel. Your sense organs are your eyes, ears, nose, tongue, and skin.

The eyes sense light and color. They send messages to the brain along **optic nerves**. The brain turns this information into a picture so we can see.

Eye

The ears sense tiny movements in the air. They send messages to the brain along **auditory nerves**. The brain turns this information into a sound.

Your nose and mouth sense chemicals in the air or in your food. The brain turns this information into smells and tastes.

Ear

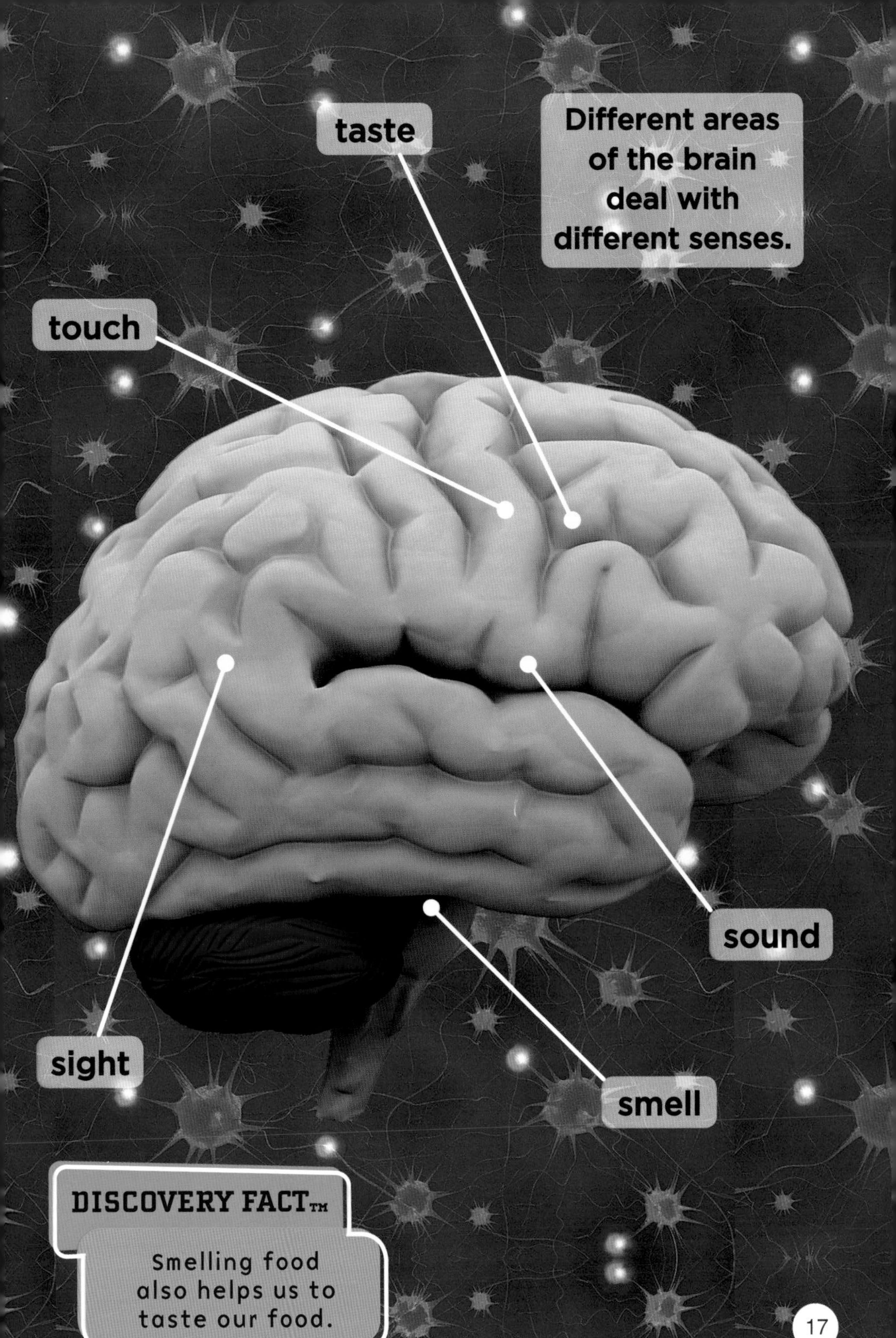

taste

touch

Different areas of the brain deal with different senses.

sound

sight

smell

DISCOVERY FACT™

Smelling food also helps us to taste our food.

DISCOVERY FACT™

Hair grows everywhere on the body, except the palms of the hands, soles of the feet, eyelids, and lips.

Skin

The skin is the body's largest organ. It is waterproof and stretchy. It protects the insides of your body from the outside world.

Tiny holes in your skin, called pores, produce sweat to help you keep cool.

Fine hairs covering your skin help to trap air. This helps you stay warm.

Melanin gives your skin, eyes, and hair their color.

The pattern of curved lines in the skin of your fingertips is different from anyone else's. It makes your fingerprints unique.

Fingerprint

Skin pores

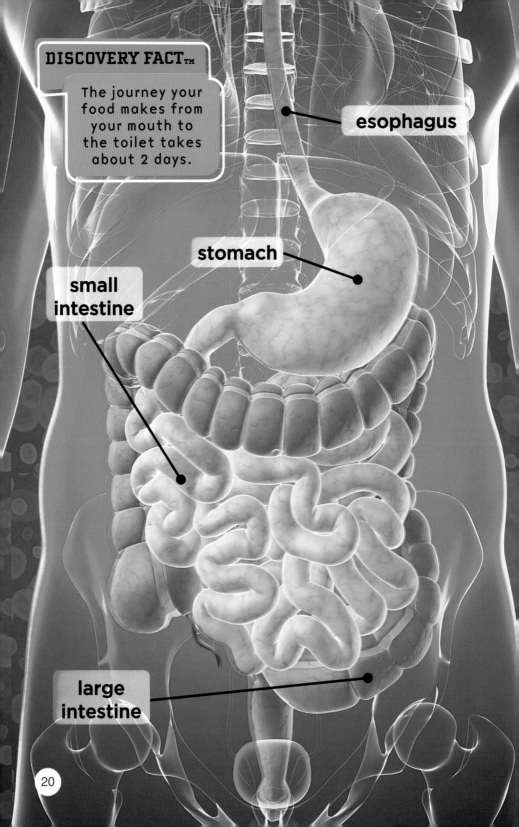

DISCOVERY FACT™

The journey your food makes from your mouth to the toilet takes about 2 days.

esophagus

stomach

small intestine

large intestine

Eating and Drinking

All the **nutrients** that your body needs to live and grow are taken from your food and drink.

Bowl of fruit salad

First, your food is turned into mush in your mouth. When you swallow, the mush goes down your esophagus, into your stomach.

Your stomach is filled with **gastric acid**. This turns the mush into a **liquid**.

Next, the liquid goes into the small intestine, where nutrients are **absorbed** into your blood.

Glass of milk

What is left goes into the large intestine, where water is absorbed into your blood and sent to your bladder. Then all that's left is **solid** waste, which goes to the bowel.

When your bowel is full, you need to poop.

Staying Healthy

Good food and exercise will keep you healthy. Even so, sometimes you get sick or hurt yourself. Luckily, your body is good at fighting sickness and mending itself.

If you cut yourself, a scab forms while your skin grows again underneath. If you break a bone, it usually takes a couple of months to mend.

Some **bacteria** and **viruses** can make you sick if they get inside your body. Washing your hands helps to get rid of bacteria on your skin. Viruses can spread through coughs and sneezes.

Scab on knee

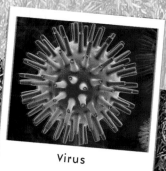

Virus

Bacteria

How Life Starts

A baby starts off as one single cell, the size of a tiny grain of sand.

A baby is made when a sperm cell from the father reaches an egg cell from the mother. The two cells join together to form one cell. Then the cell grows into a baby.

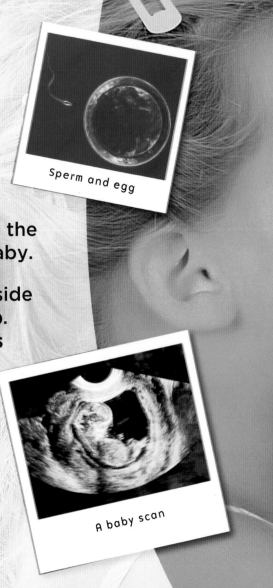

Sperm and egg

The baby grows inside the mother's **womb**. It absorbs **nutrients** and **oxygen** from the mother.

After nine months, the baby is born.

A baby scan

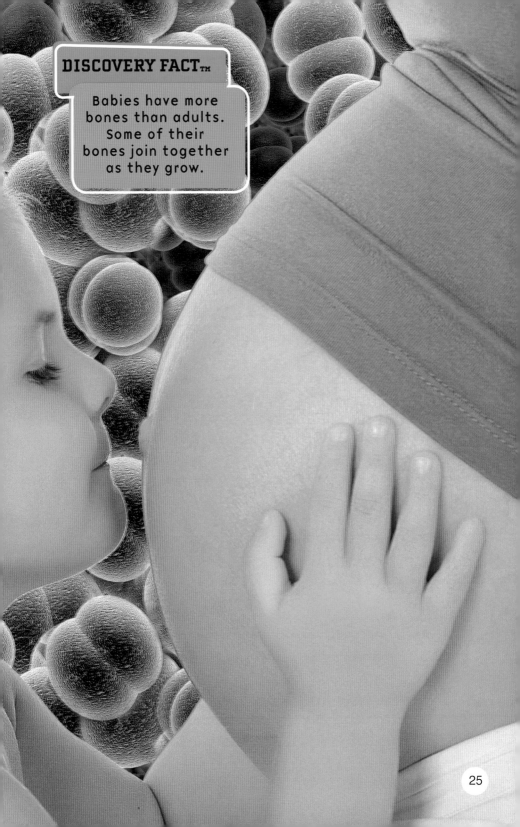

Quiz

Now try this quiz!
All the answers can be
found in this book.

1. How many bones make up
an adult skeleton?

a) 106 bones
b) 206 bones
c) 306 bones

2. Which muscle is the
biggest in your body?

a) Your biceps
   (front of upper arm)
b) Gluteus maximus
   (in your bottom)
c) Your hamstrings
   (back of thigh)

3. How do your sense organs
send messages to your brain?

a) Through your blood
b) Through the air
c) Through nerves

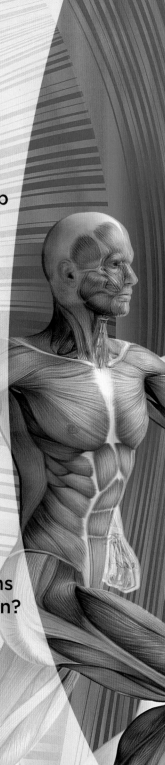

4. What is your body's largest organ?

    a) Your skin
    b) Your heart
    c) Your lungs

5. What is the large muscle under your lungs called?

    a) Abdominals
    b) Diaphragm
    c) Hamstrings

6. What does your body take from the air we breathe?

    a) Nutrients
    b) Water
    c) Oxygen

Answers: 1. b; 2. b; 3. c; 4. a; 5. b; 6. c

Glossary

Absorb   Take in / soak up.

**Auditory   The nerve that connects
nerve**   the inner ear to the brain.

Bacteria   Tiny living things that
                    live everywhere.

Gastric acid   Turns the food in our
                    stomach into a liquid.

**Internal   The organs inside your body.
organs**

Liquid   A runny substance,
                    such as water.

Microscope   An instrument used by
                    scientists to see tiny
                    objects such as cells.

Nutrients   Natural substances in food,
                    such as vitamins or minerals.

**Optic   The nerve that connects
nerve**   the eye to the brain.

Organ A part of your body that performs a special job, such as the heart.

Oxygen A gas in the air.

Sense organ An organ, such as your nose and tongue, that sends information to your brain.

Solid A hard substance.

Tendon Rubbery tissue that connects a muscle to a bone.

Tissue A type of material found in the body, made from a group of cells, such as muscle tissue.

Viruses Tiny living things that can grow only inside cells. They may make you sick.

Womb Organ inside the female body where a baby grows.

Index

Acknowledgments

Main images:
pp18-19 Getty Images/joSon
pp24-25 Getty Images/Michaela Begsteiger

All other images from Shutterstock.

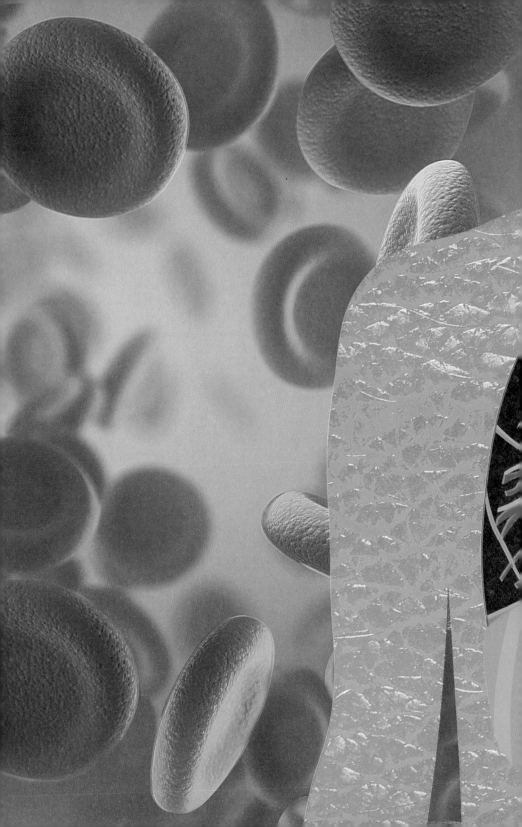